NO REGRET
COLLEGE

A GUIDE TO CHOOSING THE
RIGHT MAJOR AND MAXIMIZING
YOUR EDUCATION

DR. MARC FLEMING

Copyright © 2024 by Marc Fleming

All rights reserved. This book or any portion thereof may not be reproduced or used in any manner whatsoever without the express written permission of the publisher except for the use of brief quotations in a book review.

DEDICATION

This book is dedicated to my mom and dad for sharing their wisdom with me every step of the way.

My wife Stacey and my daughter Leah for their unyielding love and support.

All of my friends for their encouragement.

ABOUT THE AUTHOR

DR. MARC FLEMING

Dr. Marc Fleming is a professor and department chair of Pharmaceutical Economics and Policy in Irvine, California.

For the past decade, his work has involved teaching pharmacy students, including advising pharmacy resident projects. Additionally, Dr. Fleming has been involved with teaching graduate students about pharmaceutical health outcomes. Furthermore, his work with graduate students provided him with opportunities for advising/mentoring both master's and doctorate graduate students in programs across the United States. Dr. Fleming is also a well-known researcher, studying the pharmacist's role in preventing prescription drug misuse and overdose. However, his passion is mentoring students, and thus he wanted to share some of his wisdom, which only his students were privy to receiving previously.

Dr. Fleming received his Bachelor of Pharmacy from Texas Southern University and holds a Master of Public Health from Virginia Commonwealth University as well as a Master of Science and Doctor of Philosophy in Pharmacy from the University of Texas at Austin.

CONTENTS

INTRODUCTION 8

CHAPTER 1.
YOUR FUTURE MATTERS 15

CHAPTER 2.
WHY YOU SHOULD READ THIS BOOK:
A GUIDE TO CHOOSING YOUR MAJOR 18

CHAPTER 3.
THINKING ABOUT YOUR GOALS
AFTER COLLEGE 24

CHAPTER 4.
CAREER GOALS AND OUTCOMES 32

CHAPTER 5.
FINDING YOUR PASSION 42

CHAPTER 6.
PLEASE, PLEASE, PLEASE, DO THE MATH! 46

CHAPTER 7.
AFTER COLLEGE: A LOOK AT WHERE TO LIVE 52

CHAPTER 8.
AFTER COLLEGE: EXPLORING
YOUR SALARY AND BUDGET 55

CHAPTER 9.
GOOD NEWS: TIME IS ON YOUR SIDE............................61

CHAPTER 10.
ACHIEVE YOUR DREAMS: NETWORK & BUILD
RELATIONSHIPS..66

CHAPTER 11.
YOU CAN DO IT.. 73

INTRODUCTION

WHY I WROTE THIS BOOK FOR YOU

About This Book

I wrote this book for you, the high school student or early college student who is trying to figure out the best college major for themselves, and the parents of these students. After years of talking to my friends who are parents of college-aged kids and many adults who wish they could have spoken with me fifteen to twenty years earlier, this book is finally here. This book was written to change the way students go about choosing their college major. In this step-by-step guide, you will essentially work backward from thinking about the income you want to earn (e.g., how much you need to live the lifestyle you envision) to the job you will obtain to the best-fit college major.

Before we get into things, I want to first say it is perfectly fine not to be sure of what you want to do.

That is one of the reasons I was compelled to write this book—to help you figure it out.

Within this book, you will be guided step-by-step to remove the anxiety and fear and get a more assured result with your college journey. In the back of the book you will find pages for you to take notes and write down your plans or connections as you go on your collegiate journey. In my humble opinion, we put way too much emphasis on asking young people what they are passionate about when they are deciding on a career path. For me, history was always my favorite subject in school. I loved it and always made A's! As a matter of fact, I still enjoy history. I love a good documentary on US history, and as of late, I have enjoyed watching the history of food on the History Channel. However, your passions don't necessarily have to align with your career choices. Besides, most of us are only one bad boss away from looking for another place of employment or changing careers altogether. In this book, I will teach you a better way of deciding on a career and then your major for college. I will give you a method for mapping out your major area of study while gaining more clarity around the types of jobs you can do with your chosen degree of study and what type of salary you can command.

Before we get started, though, it is important for me to share why this book is so relevant and necessary. One of the primary reasons is due to my interactions with young people regarding their education as it relates to their potential careers. I would ask, "What are you planning to do with [a particular degree]?" to which some people do not have an answer. Considering the significant investment of time and money, this has been somewhat surprising to me. When I was in college, I made it a point to understand and know what I was planning to accomplish with my degree. In the early '90s, we did not have the internet, much less Google, to easily get information in real-time as is available today. I began to ponder, "Why are students not taking advantage of the internet to better understand the various careers and job opportunities?"

To provide some context from my own experiences, tuition when I started college was roughly $1,000 each semester, and in my latter years of undergraduate studies, I lived at home to save money. In 2023, depending on the state, in-state tuition can easily average $10,000 or more annually.

This does not include fees, which may vary by major, or living expenses (room and board). When considering out-of-state tuition and fees or private school education, many students and parents are paying $20,000 or more each year for tuition and fees alone. When factoring in other expenses such as food, room, and board, it can easily cost between

$50,000 and $80,000 each year to attend college. Now, I did not say all this to deter you from going to college. In fact, my hope is to encourage you to pursue college. I am a proponent of obtaining as much education as needed to accomplish your career goals, which should also give you a variety of options to explore different job opportunities.

One of my professors once shared that every time you get a degree, it is like getting a plane ticket that can take you to a new and incredible destination. That obviously stuck with me and served as a catalyst for me earning my doctorate degree. However, I must advocate researching and putting some thought into the process of choosing your major, to maximize the degree that makes the most sense for you.

As we go through the book, I will guide you through key factors using the knowledge I gained during my many years of school and as a college professor. The first thing I want you to know about me is that none of my education was easy or a breeze. Everything in this book is largely based on my experiences as a student at six different colleges and universities in two states. I have degrees from three different universities, providing me with extensive experiences in higher education from the student's perspective. Just as important, I have been on college faculty for over a decade and at three institutions, including both public and private schools. Neither of my parents received a college education, and both worked for the US Postal Service. I would consider my childhood to be a middle-class upbringing for the most part.

Getting a college education was emphasized, but more than just getting a degree, my parents were concerned with what type of job a specific degree would afford me, what type of salary my chosen major and subsequent career would provide. At one point, I changed my major to political science with the intent of becoming a lawyer.

Interestingly, I don't consider myself to be a gifted student—maybe a bit nerdy, and I enjoy learning and didn't mind putting in the long hours to achieve my education goals. Funny enough, if you asked my mom what my major was for the first two years of undergrad, she would tell you it was "fraternity." I pledged as a freshman and did enjoy a good party or two during my undergrad days. I also transferred schools and changed my major from pre-pharmacy to political science and back to pre-pharmacy before eventually being accepted into pharmacy school. Therefore, whatever you might go through or are going through, I can relate to the many challenges. Making decisions about what to study and your career path can seem like a monumental decision. Frankly, it almost doesn't seem fair to ask a seventeen-year or eighteen-year old what they want to do for the rest of their life. However, you have more control of the outcome than you might give yourself credit for, and this book is designed to show you just how to make it happen. College is about growth, maturity, and new experiences.

Though many of us travel down a curvy path as opposed to a straight line through our college experiences, as well as life, when you get that degree, you should have a good idea about where it will take you and how you want to continue from there.

At this point, I want to share a pivotal moment in my life with you. My mom never had a particularly strong concern about my progress in college, as I mainly discussed this with my dad. However, on one occasion, I shared my semester grades with her, during which time I was majoring in political science. For a social science degree like political science, the university required students to complete three social science courses outside of their specific major. Therefore, I ended up enrolling in Introduction to Anthropology. It was a fun and interesting course, and I made a good grade. I thought my mom would be proud of my good grades, but instead, she began to look pained as she asked, "Why are you taking anthropology?" I was so confused by this question, and I began to explain that I needed three social science courses for my political science degree.

"Political science!" she exclaimed. "What are you going to do with that!" I responded that I was planning to go to law school and become a lawyer and perhaps a sports agent in the future.

As my mother began to weep, I can honestly say that it freaked me out a bit. "Why is she so distraught over my career?" I thought. As much as we may hate to admit it, sometimes our parents are right. I ended up changing my major, but it took an epiphany moment for that to take place. More about that later; for now let's talk about you.

CHAPTER 1

YOUR FUTURE MATTERS

First of all, you are what matters! Your college journey is really just beginning. For parents, it is also necessary for you to understand the challenges today's students face when determining their future careers. If you are a first-generation student, finding mentors to discuss career planning is a good step in the right direction. Even if mom or dad attended or completed college, things are very different now. Thus, this book is meant to lay out a clear plan for getting you to deeply consider this all-important step that will likely dictate your future. Parents, you can't make your kids do anything they don't want to do, to some degree that is true. Forcing your child to pursue a field that you think is wise is not wrong, but there should be some compromise by both parties. Where your child goes to college is important, but more important is the area of study he or she chooses to pursue. This book is meant to serve as a guidebook for both students and parents to clearly lay out a path to climbing the financial ladder.

My late father always used to say, "You go to college to get a job!" While I recognize that it may be a bit more complex for some than it is for others, for many students, the necessity of finding employment after obtaining your degree is a real dilemma—especially if you are from a family that needs an economic contribution from you as a recent grad. This can be something as simple as your parents not having to feed and clothe you, even if you still live at home, to changing your family's income trajectory and setting up the next generation of your family with greater opportunities. And for those students taking on loans to support your educational endeavors, the ability to pay back your loans and maintain a living wage must be taken into full consideration.

While finances are one factor to consider when making decisions about college, your background, family, and friends will undoubtably have an influence as well. Each one of us has different experiences and lives in different cities that shape our views and even our goals. Perhaps your childhood friends, family, parents, or even grandparents influenced you either negatively or positively.

Some people have role models, and others have none at all. However, ultimately, we have to step back and be self-aware enough to understand who we are and what future vocation will fulfill our individual desires and dreams. We also have to overcome any limiting beliefs we may have.

If you have limiting beliefs such as, "Oh, I'll never be good at that," but it's a career that you are really passionate about pursuing, address the limiting belief first, because I am here to tell you and encourage you that you truly can be good at anything you set your mind to!

CHAPTER 2

WHY YOU SHOULD READ THIS BOOK: A GUIDE TO CHOOSING YOUR MAJOR

I want you to ask yourself three important questions. First, regardless of how excited you are about the thing you are majoring in or plan to major in, the question you have to ask is, what job will you be able to obtain with this degree? Now, my intent is not to disparage any particular major of study or discourage you from following your passion, but ask yourself, "What job will I obtain with a biology degree, a sociology degree?" If you can't answer this very important question, then you should continue reading this book. Now, there are many majors and numerous different employment opportunities, but it is critically important for you to have a good understanding of what that means for you.

Second, let's pretend for kicks that you know exactly what job you will obtain once you graduate, or you have strong idea of what job you would like to do for your career.

The second question you should ask is, "What is the anticipated salary associated with my chosen career?" If you are planning on becoming an accountant in Tucson, Arizona, do you know what the typical salary is for accountants? Money is not everything, and you certainly can't buy happiness, but one thing for sure is that happiness alone can't help you purchase the next version of the latest smartphone or cover your rent, much less pay for that vacation to Cancun. Having said that, understanding what the starting and median salaries are for the job you plan on obtaining is essential to fully realizing your return on your investment in your college education. The last thing you want to do is invest a significant amount of time and money, only to realize upon graduating and interviewing for several positions that your pay will be $40,000 per year and you have to pay rent in a city like Los Angeles. Now, $40,000 might sound like a lot of money for a new graduate who has never had a full-time job. However, during the course of this book, we will discuss more about salaries, and I will provide you with a better perspective regarding a "good salary."

The third question one must be able to answer fully is perhaps just as important as the first two questions: "What is the job demand for the job or career I plan to pursue?"

Although one can't fully know what employment opportunities will exist twenty years from now, you need to know the job outlook for the next five to ten years for your chosen career. If there are only a small number of jobs in your chosen career and many people with the same training are also looking to do the same job, why would employers need to pay a premium salary?

Now, if you can't clearly articulate an answer to all three of the questions, there is no need to worry. I will guide you through this process in a logical, step-by-step manner that will prepare you to make the best decision for you.

As I mentioned earlier, unless you come from a background of wealth and influence, it is important to understand how your major will impact your choice of employment and where you see yourself after college.

No matter what your background, if you are really passionate about something, say journalism or communications, then by all means, go for it! There is no amount of money that replaces the experience of being on assignment for a major news outlet covering major events and current headline news.

However, you must understand the probability of landing a job at a major news outlet and be willing to live with the consequences of your actions with the full realization of what opportunities you have before you and what opportunities you have forgone. That said, if you need to take out student loans or your parents have to secure loans to cover your tuition, you should consider the potential return on investment. If you invest $100,000 in your education and your income potential is $45,000 per year in annual salary, you must be conscious of the lifestyle that will afford you. At the end of the day, it is not about how much you make, but how much you plan to spend and save.

If you are still confused, don't feel stressed because you don't have to have all the answers right now! As a matter of fact, there are many forty-year-olds who don't know what they want to do.

Sometimes it seems almost unfair to ask an eighteen-year-old to decide what they want to do for the rest of their lives. The reality, though, is that you don't necessarily have to make the choice for the rest of your life, but more like for the next five years. You can take it one day at a time. You can also change your mind, much like I did. I changed majors and transferred schools, and it was not about giving up, but about finding my place.

Therefore, I want to encourage you to hold fast to your goals and dreams while understanding that transferring or changing your major is not a bad thing. Since the pandemic, many people have left their careers to pursue entrepreneurship and build brands on social media. I say to you, the sky is the limit, and part of the college experience is ultimately learning what really excites you. If you told the high school graduate me that one day I would be a professor, there is no way I would have believed it.

Take some time to think about what you plan to major in, or even consider some alternatives you might be interested in studying.

Then take it a step further by listing the actual job title you would fill with the degree you plan to consider. For example, if you plan to major in business, list the job, such as accountant, financial analyst, or social media marketer. This is an important first step, as you will build upon this first step throughout the book. This book will guide you from major, to job/career, to salary, to budget. Now let's get started by completing the table below. I am excited for you and hope you are as excited as I am about what your future holds.

Step 1: Write down three to four majors that you are considering. Next, write down the job you envision based on the listed major.

Major of Interest	Potential Job
1.	
2.	
3.	

CHAPTER 3

THINKING ABOUT YOUR GOALS AFTER COLLEGE

Pursuing Your Degree

Have you considered why you are pursuing a degree? What comes to my mind when you think about your life five or ten years from now? If you haven't given much consideration to your why, then now is the time to really consider where you see yourself.

For example, do you plan to go on to graduate school and obtain a master's degree or doctorate? Are you looking to get into a health profession program such as nursing, medicine, or pharmacy? So many times, I have talked with adults and students and asked them why they selected their chosen major and what job or career they plan to pursue once they have completed their academic program. Far too many times, they have not been able to provide a clear response. This is concerning considering the number of students with education-related debt.

However, I will not argue against investing in your own education or your child's education. This is very important and may be the key to upward mobility. The key is knowing what exactly you are investing in. I understand that there may be parental pressure to attend the school they graduated from, or you might want to go somewhere where many of your friends will be. I understand the strong influence that others can have on this very important decision. In this example, I will use anthropology, not because I don't think anthropologists are valued contributors to our society, but because I know someone who majored in anthropology and could not find a job after graduation. According to US News and World Report, anthropologists made a median salary just shy of $62,000 in 2021. In the top range of anthropologists, the salary was almost $79,000. Now, hypothetically, let's assume that you are an anthropologist making $50,000 a year, with a one-year-old child, living near a major metropolitan area. Will a $50,000 salary afford you the work-life balance and lifestyle you desire? These are the questions one must seriously consider when deciding on a career.

Your Salary after College?

The salary you can command after graduation is highly correlated with your major of study and the time in years after your degree is awarded. For example, salaries typically start relatively low for most jobs within the first two to five years but can increase substantially with raises and promotions over time.

Thus, understanding the starting salary and the median salary is necessary for gaining a clearer understanding of the current salary potential as compared to what one might expect down the road in, say, five to ten years of employment. In today's job market, workers are less likely to stay with one company for the long term.

The median number of years that wage and salary workers had been with their current employer was 4.1 years in January 2022, unchanged from the median in January 2020, the US Bureau of Labor Statistics reported today. For example, data from the Bureau of Labor found that in January of 2022, employees only stayed at their current employer for 4.1 years.

Oftentimes, moving to a new company or start-up company will give employees an opportunity to increase their salary or gain greater access to company stock.

I would be remiss to have a conversation about salary without discussing a few topics that can often be overlooked within the discussion of salary. Outside of salary, one must also consider company benefits. Employee benefits are typically not even considered until one is hired; however, benefits can greatly impact your overall compensation package. For university employees, health benefits are typically well supported by the school. Therefore, although the salary might be lower in actual pay, not having to pay high insurance premium rates per pay period might leave a higher take-home pay. Insurance deductions are not taxed. In an example where you are paid bi-weekly and your insurance deduction is $200 per pay period, that would equate to $5,200 per year in insurance premium. If your employer covered your health insurance premium, that would be the equivalent of putting $5,200 back in your pocket.

Now, one can argue that you don't need health insurance, but once you reach age twenty-six, you can no longer be carried on your parent's health insurance plan. Just as important, when you start looking at seven to ten years of being out of college and perhaps being a parent yourself, these costs factor in even more.

Lifestyle

Webster defines lifestyle as "the typical way of life of an individual, group, or culture." As students, some people try to maintain the lifestyle their parents afforded them during their years under their care. As parents, some of you are investing your hopes and dreams into your student, with the hopes that they can improve upon their lifestyle and have what you always wanted for them. Education can certainly create upward mobility, and thus, upward mobility is a measure used to rank the impact of colleges and universities.

Let's talk about salary and budget to provide some perspective to this discussion. Unfortunately, many students do not take into full consideration how their salary will dictate their budget. Now this is all about you and your financial journey. Your parents' money may not be something you can depend on long term. Also, do you want to live with your parents when you are out of college, or are you prepared to stay at home or with other family and friends who will allow you to stay with them for little to no rent? The answers to these questions will ultimately dictate your approach. Where do you want to live? What kind of car do you want to drive? How much are you willing to pay for phone, internet, Netflix, gym membership, and a host of other wants that we often view as necessities in today's society?

In the example I am about to present, you have an annual salary of $50K. According to CNBC Financial planning advice, 50 percent of your budget should be used to support your needs. These needs expenses include rent, transportation (car), utilities, internet, phone, gas, debt (e.g., student loans), food, and personal care. Some possible wants to budget for include eating out, entertainment, and new clothes.

Some amount, possibly up to 20 percent, should go toward savings or an emergency fund. In this example, $750 per month would go toward savings and $1,000 toward rent. Depending on where you live, ask yourself what type of place you can get for $1,000 per month. Is this a neighborhood in which you are willing to live? Does this mean you need to have a roommate or two? Will $400 per month be enough to cover your car expenses? Does your job provide health insurance? What other types of insurance will you need, car insurance, renter's insurance, etc.? My point here is to really have you think about the many expenses you will need to cover in your full adult life after college. Some of you might already be experienced with some or most of these bills but may still enjoy the luxury of being on your parents' insurance plan. Even if you are living with your parents, most health insurance plans do not allow you to be covered on your parents' insurance after the age of twenty-six, so that should figure into your plan.

Getting a degree should not be an exercise in pursuing the path of least resistance. Translation: nothing good comes easy.

I have seen people in my lifetime change their majors and stay at particular universities instead of transferring to different schools or taking courses at community colleges to maintain particular majors. But this is a whole other topic for a different book, so I digress. Now, let's discuss job demand. Again, in the words of my late father, "You go to college to get a job." If you major in a field with very little job demand, what are the chances of you becoming gainfully employed? Are you willing to move to a new city or state to pursue career opportunities?

Step 2: Write down the top three jobs from step one. Then list the expected median starting salary.

Top Three Jobs	Expected Salary
1.	
2.	
3.	

CHAPTER 4

CAREER GOALS AND OUTCOMES

Understanding Job Growth and Demand

In a world constantly changing and advancing, I highly recommend that you take some time to examine the job demand and job growth of your chosen career path(s). First, let's talk about job demand. Job demand can be defined as "the total number of job openings, resulting from employment growth and the need to replace workers who leave their occupation to pursue other opportunities or retirement." Job growth, on other hand, is "the projected number of job openings." These are typically presented in 5- or 10- years windows. For example, in the chart below, you will find the fastest-growing occupations in the US over the coming decade and the median pay from 2022 data.

Fastest-Growing Occupations in the United States

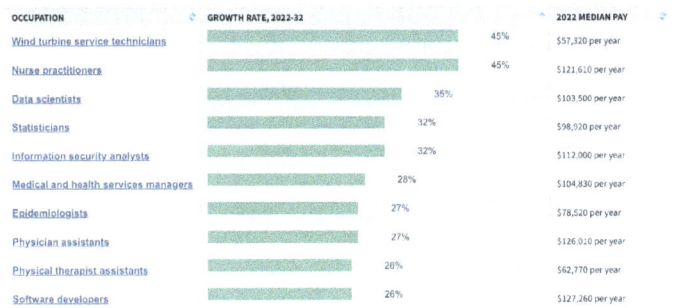

OCCUPATION	GROWTH RATE, 2022-32	2022 MEDIAN PAY
Wind turbine service technicians	45%	$57,320 per year
Nurse practitioners	45%	$121,610 per year
Data scientists	35%	$103,500 per year
Statisticians	32%	$98,920 per year
Information security analysts	32%	$112,000 per year
Medical and health services managers	28%	$104,830 per year
Epidemiologists	27%	$78,520 per year
Physician assistants	27%	$126,010 per year
Physical therapist assistants	26%	$62,770 per year
Software developers	26%	$127,260 per year

Source: The US Bureau of Labor Statistics (BLS)

If you are going to major in biology, chemistry, business, or communications but have yet to identify the actual job you want, that might be a problem. Recently, I attended an educational recruitment conference where students interested in medical and scientific graduate and medical school attended. I was surprised to encounter some students who were going to pursue a master's degree but had no clue as to what they wanted to do with the additional degree. For some, waiting until after graduation to start thinking about the job may leave them unemployed for a while after completing their degree.

Often, the focus is on maintaining grades, trying to pass and finish your degree in some predetermined number of years. There also may be financial implications, such as mom is only going to pay for one year or you need to graduate and start working.

However, what is the point of graduating to nowhere? This is a serious question that must be pondered. There are so many resources available online to obtain information on specific careers and companies. You can look at current job postings on sites like Indeed.com to get a sense of what type of background and experience some employers want you to have.

The Best Job-Growth Opportunities Today

If you are wondering where to find the best list of job opportunities, then I have some resources for you to explore. Outside of social media platforms that often interview professionals about what they do for a living and how much they make, there are not many people sharing information about job growth in the future.

Most influencers on social media are promoting or sharing information regarding their own careers. One resource that I highly recommend is the US News and World Report 100 Best Jobs list:

https://money.usnews.com/careers/best-jobs/rankings/the-100-best-jobs

The website provides the top one hundred jobs, the projected number of jobs in the future, and the median salary. Again, if you are going to college to eventually find employment, it is important to know both the job demand and potential job growth.

The site will also give you more insights into the career by providing advice on the career and some guidance on what degree to pursue for your bachelor's degree. It might also give guidance on whether a master's degree is typically needed to secure a job.

Based on the report for 2023, the #1 Best Job is software developer, with almost four hundred thousand jobs projected in the future with a median salary of $120,730. It recommends majoring in computer science and further details on other jobs one can obtain with a degree in computer science.

I can't sufficiently stress the importance of this degree and the future job demand. As we move into a world of artificial intelligence (AI) and increased demand for cybersecurity, the skills here are needed urgently as a matter of future economic growth as well as national security. The #2 Best Job on the list is nurse practitioner, with over one hundred thousand jobs projected in the future with a median salary of $120,000. To become a nurse practitioner (NP), you must first be a registered nurse by passing the National Council Licensure Examination. Therefore, it is typical for NPs to receive a bachelor's degree in nursing prior to moving into a master's program for NPs. Nurse practitioners can also receive further education and training to specialize in pediatrics or other healthcare areas, much like physicians.

For those who might want to consider a career in business or finance, the #7 Best Job listed is that of a financial manager. The projected number of jobs is approximately 123,000 in the future, with a median salary of $131,710. Financial manager is not typically a role one can obtain fresh out of college with a bachelor's degree.

Usually, majoring in finance, accounting, or economics and obtaining a Master of Business Administration will better prepare you for a role as a financial manager.

Another resource for obtaining job growth data outside of a wide Google search is the US Bureau of Labor Statistics. The US Bureau of Labor Statistics actually provides data on the top twenty occupations with the highest projected percent change in employment for the upcoming decade. Not surprisingly, nurse practitioner is the number one projected job opportunity (46 percent growth), followed by wind turbine service technicians at the number two spot (44 percent growth), commanding a median pay of $120,680 and $56,260, respectively. For comparison, at the number six spot is the occupation of data scientists (33 percent growth) with an expected median salary of $100,910. The website also provides useful information regarding what the job entails, the work environment, the job outlook, and other helpful data so you can explore geographically what the job opportunities look like across the United States.

Salary Expectations

Money is not the most important thing in life. As a matter of fact, we have all heard the saying that, "Money cannot buy happiness." This is very true. However, knowing what to expect in terms of the salary of your chosen career is important. Adulting will come with certainties, such as paying taxes, purchasing insurance for your car or home, and paying for rent, food, and so on. Therefore, having a general idea of how much money specific jobs pay is important for establishing the expectation for your income and subsequent quality of life.

Do you know how much a veterinarian makes? If you had to guess, would you say it was $70,000, or closer to $220,000? If you are like me, I would have guessed that vets make in the neighborhood of $200,000, especially since pets are so popular and common these days. For some people and families, their pet is like a child to them. Interestingly, the median annual salary for veterinarians is around $100,000. Even in the best-paying cities for vets, like San Francisco, the median salary is around $145,000 annually.

Now, I am not suggesting that you forgo becoming a vet. Clearly, we need veterinarians and they are highly respected professionals and valued members of our society. They take care of our animals and play a critical role in society.

Nonetheless, according to data from Vet School Bound, the total four-year cost for vet school ranges from the low end of $270,000 in a state like Texas to the high end in New York, with tuition totaling around $390,000.

Aside from considering what to major in, you must also consider where to pursue your education when examining the return on investment of your education. Assuming you worked for thirty years as a vet, you could reasonably expect to make close to $4 million in gross salary over the course of your career. Thus, spending $300,000 for vet school may seem like a good trade-off. I mean, the math works! However, if you spend $280,000 to get an undergraduate degree in biology before vet school and another $300,000 in loans for vet school, the math starts to work against you. The purpose of this illustration is not to discourage you from pursuing veterinarian medicine.

Indeed, if you are truly passionate about becoming a vet, I hope you pursue this endeavor wholeheartedly. Yet it is my hope that you will be very intentional about charting your educational pathway while considering the financial consequences of not only what you major in but also where you pursue your education and where you plan to live. That is not to say that if you need to be at a specific program for a particular specialty, it might be worth it for you in the long run.

Now let's look at a case of someone who majors in music. Music is valuable to our society, and I have a strong appreciation for the arts. However, a music teacher is a likely job for those majoring in music. According to Payscale.com, music teachers make about $50,000 annually in salary. Now, if you majored in music at a public university in Texas, for example, you might expect to pay $12,000 in tuition and fees ($48,000 for four years). That same music degree would cost you about $27,000 if you attended a school out of state and needed to pay out-of-state tuition at a public university ($108,000 for four years).

If looking at a private school in Texas, that same music degree might cost you closer to $50,000 in tuition before any discounts or scholarships ($200,000 for four years). Consider the five-year job growth for three occupations that you are currently considering.

Step 3: Write down the top three jobs from step one. Then list the anticipated job growth for your top three occupations.

Top Three Occupations	Five-Year Job Growth
1.	
2.	
3.	

CHAPTER 5

FINDING YOUR PASSION

Should your career represent your passion, or should your passion be supported by your career? I'm not sure about the answer to this because it's different for everyone. However, one thing is for sure—you do not want to be miserable at work. Work will take up to eight to ten hours a day minimum, so you should make sure you like what you do. The challenge here is that most of us don't know if we will really like a particular job in the future. How does one know if they will like being a doctor, much less which kind of doctor?

For many decades and at present, it seems that one may decide on a major based on one primary question: "What do you like to do or what are you passionate about?" For some the answer to this question is crystal clear. Perhaps since you were eight years of age, you knew that you wanted to be a nurse, teacher, or lawyer. Maybe you dream of being on television as a news anchor.

For students who are really clear about what they want to do for an occupation, it might be clear as to what they need to major in and the path needed.

Perhaps you have a parent or relative already working in the area of interest and you have a clear understanding of the type of work they do and the type of income one can expect. Some jobs require additional schooling, and the choice of major is less obvious or critical. For example, if planning to become a lawyer, you might major in history, political science, or psychology. If you plan on becoming a doctor, you might major in biology or chemistry to prepare for the MCAT exam.

According to Harvard University, one suggestion for better understanding a planned major of study would be to enroll in a summer course while still in high school to gain some exposure to an area of interest. One issue with the idea of your passion is that many students do not have a real sense of what they want to do. Contrastingly, some parents may feel strongly about a particular career and encourage or in some instances force students to pursue a particular career.

An important note of consideration is that even if you are passionate about an occupation, it may be more of a hobby and less than a career that affords you the lifestyle you envision. When I started college, I was passionate about making new friends and especially meeting young ladies. In fact, I was so passionate about having a social life that my mom used to tell all her friends that I was away at school "majoring in fraternity."

Step 4: Write down the top things or hobbies you are really passionate about. Then list any possible career you can envision that aligns with your listed passions or hobbies.

(It is perfectly fine if you do not have any specific passions.) You can also list pets, video games, etc.

Top Three Interests/ Hobbies	Job/Career
1.	
2.	
3.	

CHAPTER 6

PLEASE, PLEASE, PLEASE, DO THE MATH!

Maybe you haven't heard about the tragic stories of students taking on significant student loan debt and, unfortunately, being unable to pay it back. I certainly understand that college is as much an emotional decision as it is a financial decision, perhaps even more so. You have been dreaming of a certain school, and your friends are going to the same school, or perhaps your first crush. You may have heard about how great a program is, or famous faculty work there. These are all very important reasons, but you must consider the financial implications of these decisions, as they will follow you for the rest of your young career, if not longer.

In a recent survey of student borrowers, almost 55 percent felt that the debt was not worth it. Conversely, for 45 percent of students, the debt was worth it! Why do you think this split in opinions exists? Data shows that someone with a bachelor's degree will typically earn approximately $2.8 million over their career.

That $2.8 million of earned income over a career is about 75 percent more than what someone with only a high school diploma will make over their career. Now, I am not here to justify or promote that you need a degree to obtain gainful employment. However, I want you to be clearly aware that unless you plan to become an entrepreneur, you probably need a degree, and even to gain skills to become an entrepreneur, it is in your best interest to obtain at least a bachelor's degree. If you turn on an episode of The Ramsey Show (by Dave Ramsey), you will probably encounter a caller asking about what to do with all of their student loan debt. How do I pay off $250,000 of student loan debt when I only make about $70,000 per year? This is a challenge that many former students face.

Moreover, approximately 10 percent of divorces in the US are attributed to unpaid student debt. Student loan debt has also been associated with increased stress, delayed home buying, and significant feelings of being overwhelmed.

Having the ability to pay your bills and be independent will bring about some satisfaction and perhaps even some joy, regardless of the job.

Often, the entry-level position does not pay as well as senior-level positions and might seem like you are just taking orders.

However, before long, many opportunities may arise that will not only give you more autonomy on the job but may also put you in a leadership position and, yes, making significantly more income. My take-home message here is this: you and/or your parents will ultimately determine how much student debt you end up with. No one can force you to take out a loan to obtain your degree. In fact, I transferred schools after two years so I could live at home and save money. If you live in a major metropolitan area, it might be in your best interest to commute.

The reality is, even if a school knows that you may be in financial need based on your FAFSA, they have no responsibility to dissuade you from attending. Ironically, even when schools have attempted to suggest that the school might not be a good financial fit for the student, emotions often rule the day, and the student will figure out how to pay tuition, including taking on personal loans or parental personal loans (unsubsidized).

No one will tell you that if you major in music and end up with an annual salary of $35,000, you shouldn't take out $125,000 to pay tuition. These decisions are totally up to you and your parents/providers if they are in a position to assist you. Some students are totally on their own for a variety of reasons, but I don't want you to have to go it alone when making such life-altering decisions. Just as important, some careers will require a master's degree, which in many cases will bring on additional student debt.

There is good news! Some jobs provide tuition assistance or tuition reimbursement for their employees. This may be the best route for students who want to avoid significant debt while attending college. Additionally, some jobs will also support a graduate degree, such as a Master of Business Administration (MBA). I also want to point out that many STEM-related graduate degrees provide tuition support, and a stipend for being a teaching assistant.

I don't want you to walk away from reading this book and think you should not be majoring in English or music. All degrees and careers, vocations, and jobs have meaningful value in our society.

However, I am suggesting that if you decide to major in sociology or basket weaving, you need to have a clear understanding of the cost of your education and your anticipated earnings over the course of your work life.

Labor market data from 2023 showed that five years after graduation, the lowest-earning majors were as follows: theology, family and consumer services, social services, and psychology ($37,000). The aforementioned majors will allow you to earn more midcareer (increase by $20,000), but some may require you to obtain a master's degree to reach full earning potential.

Having said that, those earning a degree in finance ($60,000) and engineering ($70,000) earned considerably more in their early career and did not necessarily need to obtain more education. Some lower-paying majors, even after reaching midcareer status, did not earn as much as early career bachelor's degrees in fields that pay much higher, especially in business (e.g., finance) and engineering.

Step 4: Write down the top three colleges or universities you want to attend. If you have already decided and accepted, focus on that school. Write down the total tuition cost, assuming four years of school.

Top Three Colleges/Universities	Tuition Total (4 Years)
1.	
2.	
3.	

CHAPTER 7

AFTER COLLEGE: A LOOK AT WHERE TO LIVE

I can understand how discussing salary and budgets before you finish your college program and eventually land a job might seem a bit premature. However, please remember that in this book, we are working backward from salary to job to major. If you are not sure where you want to be, it will be more difficult to chart a path to get you there. This simple approach to mapping your career will eliminate doubt and regret. If you told me you wanted to make $400,000 per year, there are specific jobs that will practically guarantee that you make that much. It is completely within your control! Many professionals in medical sales make $300,000 or more, and many surgeons make well over $500,000 per year. Now, you may be thinking to yourself that becoming a surgeon is not something you want to do or even ever considered.

But what I want you to understand here is that you can do whatever you are willing to put forth the time and effort to achieve. You are the captain of your ship!

If you already have extensive work experience as a full-time employee, then you might be familiar with many of the topics covered in this chapter. However, if you have not worked extensively as a full-time employee with benefits such as insurance coverage, please take special note of this chapter. The topics discussed in this chapter are critical to you fully walking away with a plan after reading this book.

Have you considered how much money you will need to make to cover moderate living expenses in your city? Have you dreamed of living in New York, Los Angeles, Boston, or other major coastal cities? Whatever city you plan on living in after graduating from college, you will want to understand your salary and budget based on location. For example, the rent in Birmingham, Alabama, at the time of the writing of this book is $1,274 for a 972-square-foot apartment, according to RentCafe.com.

On the other hand, it will cost you $2,215 a month for 750 square feet in Chicago, Illinois, and $2,233 for 691 square feet in Seattle, Washington.

Step 5: Write down the top three cities you would consider living in after college. Then list the average rent for a one-bedroom apartment.

Top Three Cities	Average Rent (One-Bedroom Apt.)
1.	
2.	
3.	

CHAPTER 8

AFTER COLLEGE: EXPLORING YOUR SALARY AND BUDGET

Now this would be a good time to talk with a parent or guardian about money. Parents that are reading this book, please be open to discussing some of the household finances. Hopefully parents and/or guardians are comfortable discussing household expenses. Even if they are not comfortable discussing their salary, they may be able to give you some perspective on rent/mortgage, utilities, cable/phone, and other monthly expenses so you can gain insight into the type of life you can afford in the future. As mentioned throughout the book, the focus is not money, but for you to have a keen knowledge of planning your future. That dream car, nice apartment, or ski vacation will cost you, so planning for your future life will put you in the best possible position and help you avoid the pitfalls that beset the countless others who fail to plan.

The newest smartphone or computer is probably not going to cost you less in the future, but you will be well prepared to handle any future expenses.

Now that you have discussed household expenses with your parents or someone who is willing to share some insight, let's take a more in-depth look at a typical budget breakdown. Let's assume that your first job out of college will pay you $22.84/hr. or an annual salary of $47,500. Typically, most people get paid twice per month or bi-weekly. Some government jobs and university faculty get paid once per month, most likely on the first of the month. If we get back to our salary of $47,500, the bi-weekly breakdown is around $1,664, or $3,328 per month. As you can see, $3,328 per month does not add up to $47,500 because of the federal taxes that will be deducted from your bi-weekly check. If you happen to live in a state with no state income tax, like Texas or Florida, then your take-home pay is likely to be around $39,926. It is not uncommon for your employer to provide health insurance benefits that are partially paid for by you through payroll deductions.

Additionally, if the job has a 401(k) or other retirement savings that you take advantage of, this money will also be taken out of your take-home pay amount. In the example given, the monthly take-home pay amount can easily go from $3,328 to approximately $2,500, depending on the company and the benefit (e.g., medical insurance) structure.

Realistically, your $47,500-per-year salary can be reduced to an actual take-home pay amount ranging from $32,500 to a maximum of about $38,000, depending on where you work. The take-home message here (no pun intended) is that your salary will have deductions, and when you are building your budget and considering how you will live and play, the take-home pay is what you must work with.

Now that we have a good idea of what our take-home will be, let's build our hypothetical budget based on our future pay. I should point out that you, of course, are not limited by the one job, as it is common nowadays to have a side hustle or maybe even two. Some people drive Uber or deliver food to make extra income, while some might sell items online.

Nonetheless, we are going to build your budget based on your income from your primary job. One of the most important aspects of budgeting is ensuring you don't spend what you don't have. If you spend more than you bring in, you most likely are incurring credit card or other debt. As a new grad, you have other options to save money, such as taking on a roommate, renting a room in a home, or just staying with family.

According to Erin Michelle Sky for Quicken, one can have approximately twenty items that need to be budgeted on a monthly basis. We will assume a take-home pay of $2,691 per month.

Financial planners often recommend the following regarding the budget breakdown of the different categories (e.g., rent, transportation):

Housing/rent – 30 percent

Utilities – 10 percent

Food (including takeout) – 15 percent

Transportation – 10 percent

Insurance (medical, renters, home, auto) 10–25 percent

Clothing – 5 percent

Entertainment and travel – 5–10 percent

Savings – 15 percent

Using an online budget planning calculator tool, you can get a great idea of what your future budget would look like. Using the example of someone making $42,000 per year in annual gross salary, that would be equivalent to $35,507 after taxes and around $2,691 per month, assuming that you do not have any other deductions coming out of your check, such as retirement savings and insurance premiums. Another way to simply think about budgeting is to use the 50/30/20 method.

In this method, using $2,600 monthly take-home pay, you would have $1,300 for needs, $780 for wants (e.g., clothes, entertainment), and about $520 for savings or paying down debt.

If you live in a state that has a state income tax, then you will have to account for that state tax deduction in your check. For example, in Illinois, you would bring home about $700 less per month based on state income tax deductions.

Step 6: Using your anticipated annual salary, use an online calculator to find your monthly take-home pay. Then list your amounts based on the 50/30/20 method.

Do not forget to account for state income taxes, depending on where you plan to work.

Budget (50/30/20)	Allotted Amount ($)
Needs	
Wants	
Savings/Debt Repayment	

CHAPTER 9

GOOD NEWS: TIME IS ON YOUR SIDE

I want you to know that time is truly on your side. If the things shared about budgeting are overwhelming, don't let them be! Adulting comes with its own set of challenges, no matter who you are or your income bracket. Also, I don't want you to be discouraged about what to major in if you are still undecided. If you are truly passionate about your goals and dreams, then focus on that. If you know exactly what you want to accomplish, then move forward with steadfast vigor. This book was meant for all students to consider and also to help parents have some tough conversations and insight into some of the challenges that students face today. My goal for you is that this book and the information within can contribute to setting you on a strong economic path, as compared to facing a lifetime of unsurmountable debt and regret. The beautiful thing about life is that you can always pivot. It is just easier to pivot from the position of a stronger financial foundation.

Some people have a career trajectory that moves in a straight line. For others, me included, it is more like a figure eight on the bottom of a triangle.

I changed my major from pre-pharmacy to political science and then back to pre-pharmacy. I was sitting in a geography class as part of my social science requirement. I thought to myself, this class will be an easy A, so I enrolled. I remember that day as if it was yesterday. I had given up on pharmacy because organic chemistry was destroying my confidence as a student, not to mention ruining my social life. I decided that I was going to get a degree in political science, with a plan to eventually go to law school. I thought I might teach history during the time between graduation and law school.

The professor walked in on the first day of class and promptly went into a monologue about how some students were in his class for the wrong reasons. He said, "Some of you are here for an easy A." I was like, "WOW, is this guy talking to me?" as I looked around the classroom (more like a small auditorium).

Then he talked about how you might get hired to be a teacher, but what you teach will be dependent upon the needs of the school district. You might be thinking that you want to teach eighth-grade social studies but might end up teaching tenth-grade world history. I felt like this man was speaking to me directly. It was at that very moment that it hit me: "No matter what I major in, no degrees are handed out."

Some may be less challenging to obtain, but I knew that I wanted to chart a more certain path, and I was confident that pharmacy would be the best choice for me. Pharmacy promised great job demand and growth and a great salary. Not only that, but being a respected professional and helping others was very appealing to me. When I entered pharmacy school, pharmacists were considered some of America's most trusted professionals (second behind nurses). I left that class and immediately went to the registrar's office to change my major back to pre-pharmacy. It was a pivotal moment in my life and put me on the path to becoming a pharmacist and, many years later, a pharmacy professor.

If you are truly passionate about something like journalism, business, acting, or music, then pursue any topic you are really passionate about. In the long run, passion will win out! For me, once I decided to pursue graduate education, I was passionate about it. I gave up full-time pharmacy employment (a six figure salary) to go back to school and work part-time. I always told myself to follow my passion and the rewards would come. I know it sounds cliché, but I wholeheartedly believe this.

For example, actress Angela Bassett, of Black Panther fame and a long list of other movies and TV roles, attended Yale University and pursued a Master of Fine Arts degree, much to the dismay of her parents. But she held fast to that dream, using her passion and determination to become a leading Hollywood actress. Bobby Flay, of cooking fame, dropped out of high school at the age of seventeen to pursue his culinary passion. Now Bobby Flay is one of the most recognized chefs in North America.

You can become anything you want, and obtaining an education is still a great way to be a positive contributor to your community and family while making enough money to live comfortably.

In my view, getting your education gives you a fantastic opportunity to narrow down the vast number of career choices and find a path to earn income to support your needs.

Time is on your side! I went back to school to pursue my PhD at the age of thirty-five. It is never too late, and you can have as much education as you want to complete, but that education should not leave you in uncertain debt that feels impossible to overcome. If you are in a position where you need to earn a decent income to take care of yourself and/or others, whether a child, sibling, or parent, I hope that you will take into consideration the return on your investment in your education.

CHAPTER 10

ACHIEVE YOUR DREAMS: NETWORK & BUILD RELATIONSHIPS

Although this book is primarily focused on choosing a career based on understanding the financial impact it will have on not only you but also your family, I want to give you some advice that is useful for students and adults at any stage of their careers. You hear about networking all the time. So many sayings exist about networking: "Your network is your net worth" (Porter Gale), and "It is not what you know, but who you know" (unknown), to share a couple. One of your primary goals on your road to success in any endeavor is to build genuine relationships. When I speak to my students, I emphasize that this is not networking. I do not refer to this "relationship building" as networking because most of us, including you, are most likely not running a business. At least, that is not what this book is about.

In my view, when people think of networking, images of a businessperson or salesperson may come to mind—the idea that you are connecting in exchange for something in return.

I want to move away from this term when communicating with students, and I will explain this concept further by employing examples from my own experiences.

I have been fortunate to have family, friends, professors, supervisors, colleagues, and classmates help me along the way. My next-door neighbor, who graduated high school two years before me, told me this: "Don't be just a college student." In other words, get involved in organizations or clubs during your time in school. Some opportunities may come from meeting the right people and building a well-rounded resume, including volunteering. For many students, there will be challenges on your journey toward academic achievement and job seeking. However, building relationships with other students and other campus leaders will assist you tremendously in many instances.

Now, that doesn't mean that you must join a sorority or fraternity, but you should get involved in organizations or clubs that interest you. Numerous campus clubs and organizations exist, from chess club, cultural groups, and student government to intramural sports and so on. Take these opportunities to build relationships with your peers.

What about faculty and staff, you ask? Yes, university staff and faculty are very important on your journey.

I will speak about this from my own experiences as a student. If you were to ask me about my personality thirty years ago, I would describe myself as shy and reserved. I did fine in social settings with my peers, but I did not like talking with adults, much less authority figures like my professors. I soon realized that I needed to break out of my shell to reach my full potential. This will require you to be vulnerable. Vulnerability is so, so scary, but if you need help, who will know better than you? There is NO SHAME in asking for help, especially from your professor. I was struggling with a math course and began to seek the advice of my professor.

I went to the professor at the end of the semester to discuss my final grade and ask if he could round up my average to the next letter grade (not to get an A). I had met with this professor about three times previously during the semester, so he knew me!

There might have been fifty students in that class, but he knew me. I told him that I wanted to get into pharmacy school one day and that this course was essential. He told me that he could not give me any more points, but he would be happy to write a letter of recommendation to pharmacy school when I was ready to apply. I thought to myself, "This is both good and bad at the same time." Although I did not get the points I was seeking, my math professor had just offered to write me a letter of recommendation. I am pretty sure that his letter was one of the key factors that got me accepted into pharmacy school.

Now, I realize that not all professors are like the one mentioned in the previous section. Unfortunately, some may be unfriendly, uninviting, or just plain rude. Please do not put yourself in any uncomfortable situation or allow anyone in authority to take advantage of you in any way.

Also, if you encounter a situation where a professor is not helpful, please do not be discouraged. During my time in school, I encountered a professor who offered no help when I was struggling, so I understand the difficulty you may face. However, I want to encourage you to be undeterred in your academic success. Do not be embarrassed or dejected if you need to drop a class and sign up with a different professor in the next term.

If you are planning to get a job or apply to graduate or professional school, a letter of recommendation will undoubtedly carry the most weight. As a pharmacy professor who has reviewed my share of applicants as well as participated in interviews for pharmacy school, the letters of recommendation matter, especially the ones written by a professor of a core required course in math, biology, or chemistry. Even in pharmacy, I ask my students in their second year of our program if they know who they would ask to write them a letter of recommendation if they needed one.

Now, let's get back to the concept of relationship building. Building relationships, simply put, is nothing more than getting to know people, but also, importantly, letting people know you. This can be sharing your aspirations, fears, and challenges. I can tell you that without my professors' support, I would not have obtained four degrees. I will not go into every single person and example because, honestly, I could probably write more than a few Chapters about the emotional support I have received along my journey. However, there is one story that I want to share that still makes me a bit emotional just thinking about it. When I applied to graduate school at the University of Texas at Austin, one of my previous pharmacy professors who I asked for a letter of recommendation called my program.

You read that correctly! She called the program on my behalf and vouched for me. Let that sink in for a moment. That is what building relationships looks like. That is also what caring professors will do to see their former students move forward to new levels of achievement. There is a difference between building relationships and networking.

Building relationships is not about what the person can do for you, and truthfully, you typically do not know which people in your life will ultimately become your biggest advocates and mentors. Just know that when they do, it is because of the relationship you have built with them by getting to know them and letting them get to know you.

Everything I have shared about building relationships is from my own lived experiences. I was never a straight-A student, so the support came from professors who could see my drive, desire, and passion and what I call my "want to." If you have that "want to," want to contribute to society, want to help people, want to be successful, want to achieve your dreams, the people you build relationships with will see it very clearly. Unfortunately, we sometimes walk away from or even avoid our blessings. During my doctoral training, I avoided my advisor for about six months. In my mind, she was way too demanding. During that time, I was working many hours outside of school and therefore was not mentally prepared to handle the demands. However, she turned out to be a key mentor and advocate for me, and I owe much of my success in academia to her guidance and mentorship.

CHAPTER 11

YOU CAN DO IT

As I conclude this book, I want to encourage you to follow your dreams. The reality is like many things in life, like eating healthy or being an elite athlete: hard work is necessary to achieve certain heights. Honestly, when you consider medicine, science, and other technical fields of study, being good at what you do is important to ensure public safety. You can't have engineers or architects laying out plans that lead to unstable infrastructure. Therefore, the appreciation for those with the focus and patience to endure rigorous academic pursuits is warranted. No matter what you plan to pursue, there may be difficult challenges along the way. Take those opportunities to build your resilience and grit, and keep pressing forward.

We need you to achieve your goals and become the future nurses, doctors, engineers, psychologists, etc. Education is a great tool and a privilege that should not be taken for granted.

Some students are forced to attend by parental pressure, while some wish they could attend but may not have the funding or need to work to support the family. Therefore, if you are able to attend college, please make the most of the opportunity and don't forget to have some fun and enjoy the experience. College was so fun and edifying to me that I ultimately decided to pursue graduate education and the goal of becoming a college professor.

There may be some challenges along the way. Some paths do not follow straight lines, but do not be deterred. Some majors are more rigorous academically than others. Whatever you decide to study, know that you can accomplish your goals as long as you are focused. If it was easy, everybody would choose the path you intend to pursue. Embrace obstacles, learning opportunities, and experiences that build character. The obstacles you overcome on your journey will serve to make your accomplishments that much sweeter in the long run. I can tell you from my own experiences, especially while pursuing my doctorate, that things were, at times, difficult. In pharmacy school, I also faced some challenges and obstacles along the way. However, graduating is an amazing feeling, and when I look back at my time as a student, I feel thankful for those experiences.

The experiences, the challenges that I overcame, and the people I met along the way have served me well in the journey of life. Lastly, I want to wish you the very best in whatever you decide to pursue. Remember, you can, you can, you can accomplish your dreams!

THE END

NOTES

NOTES

NOTES

NOTES

NOTES

NOTES

NOTES

NOTES

NOTES

NOTES

NOTES

NOTES

NOTES

NOTES

NOTES

NOTES

NOTES

NOTES

NOTES

NOTES

NOTES

NOTES

NOTES

NOTES

NOTES

www.ingramcontent.com/pod-product-compliance
Lightning Source LLC
Chambersburg PA
CBHW070307230526
45470CB00002B/763